D0014420

A Gift for

....

From

....

You can't return this.
I licked it!

Cats and Dogs Unleashed
Pets with Attitude!

Copyright © 2004
Hallmark Licensing, Inc.

Published by Hallmark Books, a division of Hallmark Cards, Inc., Kansas City, MO 64141
Visit us on the Web at www.Hallmark.com.

Editorial development: Jane-Elyse Pryor
Art Director: Mark Cordes
Designed by: Kendra Inman (with inspiration from Luna and in memory of Muffy)

The people minds behind the pet minds: Linda Barnes, Trish Berrong, Chris Brethwaite, Keely Chace, Lottie Chestnut, Dorothy Colgan, Suzanne Heins, Carolyn Hoppe, Ginnie Job, Mary Loberg, Diana Manning, Derek McCracken, Lisa Riggin, Alarie Tennille, Mary Miro, Linda Staten, Myra Zirkle, Dierdra Zollar

Photographers behind this "pet project": Todd Balfour, David Biegelsen, Scott Gibbons, Kevin Hosley, Don Lesko, Ninette Maumus, Ken Sabatini, Lisarae Turnbull-Oliva, Walt Whitaker, Steve Wilson (except select stock used on cover and pgs. 2, 3, 6, 7, 26, 32, 35, 40, 56, 60, 71, 77, 88, 102, 103)

Printed in China
BOK2051

GIFT BOOKS
from Hallmark

Cats and Dogs Unleashed

Pets with Attitude!

Oh, please don't look at me like that.
Why, all I did was chase the cat!
All right—I also chewed your shoes,
And in your chair I took a snoozzzze!
Now I know I'm in disgrace.
(Can't you tell that by my face?)

I've analyzed the problem,
Now my course of action's clear...
It's time to call for help—
Somebody get me down from here!

DOGGIE WISDOM:
From ancient hound to tiny pup,
let this truth be known:
He who is too proud to beg
never gets the bone.

Good-bye! Have fun! I'll take good care.
Don't fret about one thing!
Just let me stalk...er...sit right here
And watch the birdie swing!

I'm in to shredding pillows.
I know I'm such a brat.
The reason that I do it
Is they always blame the cat!

A crash? I don't know what you mean.
I guess I didn't hear it.
And if you find a broken vase,
I'll swear I wasn't near it!

Oh goody, a party—
What joy and excitement.
I can't tell you how much that **thrills** me.
And don't I look festive?
You owe me for this!
I guess I'll have fun…*if it kills me!*

Although I hear you calling,
I'm not budging from this place.
Kitty-kitty's not my name…
And I don't like your face!

Princess snoozes
wherever she chooses!

I wasn't made for labor
or for any kind of strife.
I much prefer a kitty's
carefree, comfy, cushy life.

I know I'm quite adorable—

that's why you can't resist
receiving doggy kisses from
a handsome mug like this!

I have a certain type of build.
Let's see now, what's the word?
Some might call me heavyset,
but I prefer **big-furred.**

Lean,
MEAN
Leftover
Machine.

I am cunning,
I am bold,
Sleek and stunning
to behold.
Fierce and fearless
through and through—
I am kitty...
hear me mew!

Can Scout come out and play?

We won't harass a single cat.
(I'm already in the doghouse
for some other stuff like that!)

Smelling something putrid
wafting through the house?
Perhaps the couch is not the place
to bury a dead mouse!

It's my turn now! Let's see how far
You can run to catch the car!

Take it from me, Kid,
 you've gotta wise up
if we're gonna be **partners in crime.**
 Just sittin' there
  lickin' your whiskers like that
 is a dead giveaway every time!

Reckon, Son, it's time you learned
this here's an indoor tree.
It's not a place where you can lift
your leg and take a...

Well, you know, take care of business!

Pure kitty joy—a tree indoors
with balls on every limb...
and Kitty's sure that every one's
a play toy just for him!

They threw our paper in a tree,
        and how to get it baffled me.
But fetching this one wasn't hard—

        I got it from the neighbor's yard!

(She's coming! Act innocent!)

What do you mean

    the two of us just can't be trusted?

Of course we weren't ordering

                Anchovy pizza...

(Stop dialing already—we're busted!)

I'm tired and grumpy,
plus bored to the bone.
So take off this hat

and then leave me alone!

Every nook and cranny
just has to be explored,
No cardboard box or grocery bag
can ever be ignored...
Every top of, underneath,
and inside must be tried
Before our curiosity
is fully satisfied!

If you want my sole attention,
      it's a pretty simple feat—
Just settle on the sofa
        with a plate of food to eat.

We have double the fun
as we shred drapes and run,
as we frolic and jump up on laps.
So don't think us rude
if we go on and snooze...
'Cause we also need double the naps!

Your couch? Well, if I broke the rules,
excuse my indiscretion!
But seems to me the couch is mine
when I'm in full possession!

I was here first,
and don't you forget it...
You get any closer,
and you might regret it.

Some say I've got a regal air—
Sophisticated, debonair;
So dignified, so cultured, and so couth.
I try to blush and disagree
And thinly feign some modesty,
But who am I to argue with the truth?

I'm really not so hard to please,

as princess kitties go—

Just put me on a pedestal

and curtsy nice and low!

Why'd you have to do it…
      make me wear this silly hat?
I look so darn ridiculous,
      you'd think I was a cat!

...so I sez to the mutt,
"Oh, yeah? You and whose army?"
I bared all my fangs,
and I stuck out my claws.
He turned tail, this pooch,
and then started running...
So don't call me Fluffy,
from now on, it's...Jaws!

I snarl and growl and glare
at everyone who passes by—
I hope they never guess
I wouldn't even hurt a fly!

Don't worry—I'm just looking.
These fish are safe with me.
Silly, wriggly, drippy things
just aren't my cup of tea.

In case you're the only one
left on the planet
who hasn't heard
"can't teach an old dog new tricks,"

I wanna make sure
you don't get no ideas
like havin' me jump up
and run after sticks!

Yes, I'm a big, fat puddy cat,
   but put ME on a diet?
         You see this face?
I'll trash your place—
      that low-cal crud don't buy it!

Who's the fairest of them all?
I needn't even look!
'Cause when it comes to fabulous...
my dear, I wrote the book.

You think I'm a dandy?
Well, I've got some news.
The last cat who called me that
lost all his mews.

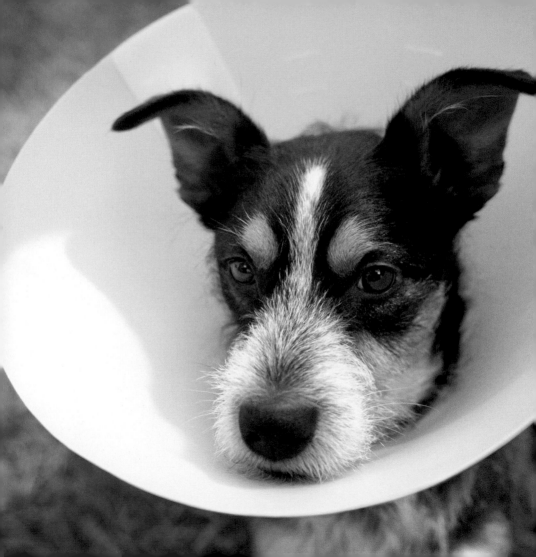

It shouldn't happen to a dog!
It's more than I can bear!
This collar is the ugliest
I've ever had to wear!

Some say cats are too conceited,
much too **pampered,** too well treated.
I don't let that bother me—
I write it off as jealousy.

I've almost got my master trained
          (Of course, he doesn't know it),
Each time I bring the ball to him,

He'll pick it up and throw it!

On sleepy, lazy afternoons
when no one's home but me,
I curl up on a pillow
and escape reality.

This brand-new rule
   of "wipe your feet"
        has got me so perplexed—
I s'pose she'll send me out
   with my own pooper-scooper next!

I just love to take a catnap
with a buddy of my choosing—
Cuddled up, our paws entwined...
the very best in feline snoozing!

A dog will be
your friend
to the end!

We'll always be the best of pals,
but don't tell anyone—
they'll say that dogs and cats should fight
instead of having fun!

We hope this book has made you smile

And kept you entertained awhile.

Perhaps your pet enjoyed it too?

If so, we'd like to hear from you!

So please feel free to **send us mail,**

The "e" kind if you wish, or "snail."

Book Feedback

2501 McGee, Mail Drop 250

Kansas City, MO 64141-6580

booknotes@hallmark.com